Inexhaustible Life of Chaos

Poetry of
Angst & Anger

ROBEC ENTERPRISES, LLC
St. Robert, Missouri

For permission requests, write the author, addressed "Attention: Permissions" at recoverywise@gmail.com
Or visit www.recovery-wise.com for more information

ISBN: 9780578816951
Printed in the United States of America
Set in CRT Garamond

This anthology has previously appeared on the author's website
www.recovery-wise.com

10987654321

FIRST EDITION

To Those

who taught me angst
who taught me anger
who wrote words herein
you will find no stranger

To Anna,
All The Best!

Rob

Table of Contents

Table of Contents

Angst

Anger

ANGST

Suffocate Me

Seep slowly into my core
it is you I desperately adore
filling my soul with wonder.

Suffocate me on this night
ominous mist of dark delight
deep trance I have fallen under.

Slowly blind me with your lies
so surely sweet intention dies
this mind is cast asunder.

Does this truly thus portend
an aching dying sorry end
your spell I have fallen under.

Thus, my promise laid to waste
surely chasing illusions taste
this love casts hope asunder.

This lying love screams disdain
loudly echoes her death refrain
torments my soul with wonder.

Wires Crossed

Oh this clinging
is stinging
out of my element
not my temperament.

I am adrift
on this stormy ocean
in wonder and in
adoration wires crossed.

I have lost my mind
loving deep
losing sleep
tossing turning.

This anguish burns
ignites a fire
losing my balance
navigating a tripwire.

I need to cope
to avoid more
sliding down this
slippery slope.
⏹
Save me from
sweet rhapsody
such as this
sweet blinding bliss.

Why am I
holding on so tight
my wires crossed
feeling lost.

-Wires Crossed-

Oh, my love
I am naked
with need
desperation freed.

I am raw in this
feeling
reeling
do not run from me.

It is just this
love is angst
is ecstasy
my wires crossed
emotions lost.

Never

Of past regrets
I know too much
and echoes which
sounded like sin
I know too well
that frozen touch
which I will never
ever feel again.

White Door

A cold white door
not in my home
a key
golden hope
not in her hand.

The cold pale room
not in my dreams
who could have
known
not in my mind.

Outside the vengeful
wind blows angry
and inside we
shiver my numb
hands shake.

Cold white folds
adorn white curves
pressed against
the idea we gasp.

Aged in a moment
the deception revealed
a parting gift
and a parted loss
is all I know.

A Thousand Times

You would not enter my room
my fear landed on your lips
thoughts without words were
easily seen though reserved
within your cast down eyes.

Your words like molasses
slipped achingly slow
from sticky lips as the
softest hands I ever knew
clutched my reluctant ones.

Bitter is the kiss that
is cold and consolatory
that weakly disguises the
pretense of enduring affection
in its cool brevity.

And your intoxicating scent
sweet residue on my cheek
would not wash away
under the flow of tears
my valor failed to defeat.

Even your crooked smile
would not erase the image
of those taillights those
blurry globes a thousand
times over regret could
never replace the loss.

You Left Me

You were to stay
on the eve of our love
you left me
to live desolate
within dark days.

It is not clear
the whys of your ways
you left me
while I lived
to love you.

Dreary is the
cold grave of grief
frigid its embrace
you left me
to ache bereft.

Imbued with angst
never telling me
the whys
of your ways
so I cling
to the sting
of happier days.

Unspoken

Draw sad pastel scene
a brief paint just to show
stains to make me wonder
why I let her go.

Feel my woeful lines
a love verse made for you
thoughts to cast asunder
what you thought you knew.

Hear the music's score
a love tune made you sway
notes as loud as thunder
wish I had you stay.

Pen this last quatrain
a love poem just to show
words now share my blunder
words you can never know.

Illusion Delusion

Smash this glass
her fantasy so magically
is captured for all time
who transfixes me
in idolatry this love
within my rhyme.

A thousand miles
I would traverse
just to taste your skin
but then my dear
I do fear I would never
come back again.

From the thrills
the wonder the spills
the thunder
your heaven would ignite
so then I would lose
a thousand hours
dreaming every night.

Smash this glass
this fantasy that makes
me think you are near
thus away my happy day
spent in this dream
I am afraid I fear.

York

The chill breeze of
May at the beach
was scarcely warmed
by the dull gray sun.

How your hair danced
jovially around your face!

How sweet was your kiss
as we embraced at York.

The beach is barren in
April on my page though
memories bring back
the love that raged.

No more do voices sing
in our hearts at York
and on the page these
lines changes the memory.

October Day

I still remember that October day
how the wind swept leaves away.

The noon sun glorified raven hair
how it flowed how I had to stare.

Painful memories refusing to die
for many years I wondered why.

Why cruel winter rueful and gray
bleak and pitiless stole you away.

Yet constant as the crescent moon
remembrances of love are strewn.

Forever I think on an October day
when the wind swept leaves away.

Blind Romance

The wind it howls
through the trees
as I am crumpled
on wounded knees.

My mind is lost
to the sky
mingles with you
way up high.

Time is thieving
stealing days
rotting my hope
so love decays.

My soul tormented
through the years
suffering silence
burn my tears.

The wind it howls
through the night
scatters careless
my loveless plight.

I seek the courage
I seek the chance
to run and embrace
this blind romance.

Again and Again

Sensuality of you that touch
reaches me affects me much
I drift I dream a heavy sleep
lilac memories mine to keep.

Sunshine hope is burning bright
but this loving belongs to night
yearning for you from long ago
today am still wanting you so.

Snow is falling so gently outside
by logic my heart will not abide
though we parted in sorrow and pain
you torture my soul again and again.

A Particular Pause

How a long-lost love becomes forgotten
during a resonant lonely pause on a piano
and any note sounding a remembrance
ceasing a certain pause on a particular piano.

The utter beauty of haunting notes…whispers
of their love from that sweet April night
lulling and comforting this lingering music
lingers and envelops a forlorn lover.

And (ever present and ominous) a particular
pause on a certain piano harkens their fate
so go cherished fading memories as the
present is no longer eclipsed by what was.

Cast away

Cast away this
little poem
beyond the icy brook.

Cast away this
fairy tale
from a children's book.

Toss away this
silly dream
from the dead of night.

Toss away the
lovely girl
from your bleary sight.

Cast away this
ancient chant
from your memory.

Cast away this
little poem
beyond frozen tree.

Heaven and Hell

Long lilac grace
brave bold embrace
familiar dread face
I know.

Serene soft kiss
feeling fine bliss
tame tenderness
I think.

Holding hot chance
calming close glance
daunting vague dance
I know.

Weary worn eyes
divulge dead whys
long imagined lies
I think.

Trite terse dream
languid love's theme
sad imagined scheme
I know.

Damned Soul

Damned soul
that torments me
visions of her.

Stoic they stay
never did I
ask for our
sacred memories
to haunt me.

Damned soul
allow my psyche
respite a reprieve.

From my reveries
never had we
awakened fully
the love that
raged in us.

Alone upon a
bleak island
lies my soul
despairing there.

Despair

D
esolation tears are streaming
E
viscerated thoughts are teaming
S
orrow sadness rules my dreaming
P
athos tragic to which I am bound
A
nguish deep I bleed on the ground
I
mmeasurable loss of love I found
R
egret and horror it is seeming.

Desolate Sadness

Thought I knew
what love was
until there was
you.

Now that you are
gone I see what
is true.

Love severs your soul
love runs you through.

My tears are raining
staining all that I see
such depths
of despair oh this agony!

My heart is shattered
battered tattered
torn
desolate anguish
within me is born.

I flew too high to the
sun like Icarus, I have
come undone.

Withering dying
moaning sighing
wailing crying
cannot grasp reality
cannot accept this
casualty.

-Desolate Sadness-

Crushed and broken
words unspoken
you simply pivoted
tore away
never turned back
nothing to say.

Death of love
so alone
my heart obliterated
I turn to stone.

ANGER

Shattered Prisms

Who is this I have found
lying dying on the ground
drowning in her prose and woes
making not one single sound?

Where does she go to
where does she hide
see how she is swimming
against a recondite tide?

Corrupt with despair
her broken being
her petrified stare
shattered prisms
that I am seeing?

Such seems her duty
moonlit soliloquy
mourning such losses
aching for her history
ever aimless to and fro
furiously seeking yet
blind in the snow.

Where does she go to
where does she rest
is she imprisoned
within her own breast?

Dare not intend to
scour this stain
from her smashed
and broken brain
sadly sit and watch
this show transcendent
to hell will we go.

-Shattered Prisms-

Where does she go to
where does she sleep
see how she is locked
in the creature's keep.

Who is this I have found
rotting degrading
into penury fading
choking on the
bloodied inexorable sands
of her once so
pristine inviolable lands?

A Call to Arms

There did not have to
be a reason no one thing
no trigger
it was always boiling
just beneath the surface
always.

It could have been
the number of nips
lying empty on the desk
next to the ashtray.

You know the one
the one that left
the two scars
the one which you
hurled in anger
and in rage
with hostility
and hopelessness.

I could always tell
when Adele was
playing in the car
the hours will not pass
quickly no
it will be a long night
a call to arms
a call in the morning
"I won't be in today
something's come up."

Bad blood would
ooze from the
downturned corners
of your filthy mouth

venom and disdain
from hateful eyes
from chewing on
the razors of your
merciless
rage and despair.

So many
candle impressions
left on walls
breaking windows
staining chairs
so many treasures
and keepsakes shattered.

Amazing how you
were always ready
for a new scene
how you managed to
replace the facts
change the clues
change impressions
replace the views.

But then you were
exceptional at
appearances the mess
outside scrubbed tidy
(inside would always
be ugly spiteful vengeful).

You were so thorough
so occupied with
blinding yourself
through your efforts
to your ugliness.

-A Call to Arms

Not me could not
clean this mess
filthy with horrors
dirty with dread
scummy with fear
on the inside
never knowing when
the other heel
was going to drop
or when the police
would reappear
skeptical again
breathing the stagnant
air of violent depravity.

In the end you wrote a play
I was the unknowing lead
the irony the comedy
the blasphemy
great theatre
it did not win me awards
what a drama!

Your performance epic
your sad woman's show!
No sweat I took on
the bout no man could
win no sweat
it was the principle of it
I was not lying down.
But the judge she did not
see it my way
funny that k'od.

But now! But now!
I have today

-A Call to Arms-

freedom never
tasted so good
sometimes I am amazed
that I do not
have more scars
but then again
your aim was never
really that good
was it?

Bitch

So mangy
is the dog
that nips
at my heels
matted fur
wet with a
bitter stench.

Her eyes
half guilty
half wanting
always needing
a morsel
of kind remembrance
staunch in her
pursuit.

Go away bitch
turn that
ragged ass
around
and slink back
into
your cold
and lonely
and jealous
domain.

There is no treat
for you here.

I always loved
cats best
at least
you know when
your life

-Bitch-

breaks free
they could
give a shit.

You can
find them on
the windowsill
on a warm
and
sunny day
funny that
is where I am
we are and
you are not.

Fresh Torrent

Their relevance defunct
this romances brevity
could not even warrant
a freshly cut torrent.

Cookie cutter words so
carefully cut and pasted
on me are simply wasted.

Thoughts on you only
today are freshly writ
not someone else's skit.

Your cycle oft repeated
new color same game
please shame and blame.

Faded far from view
a barren desolate land
this love's final stand.

Pain is public domain
burn your copyright
cliché it into firelight.

Blank page tattered torn
crumpled piss-stained
empty promises drained.

Program pre-recorded
tired hackneyed phrases
sung too long the praises.

"the lady doth protest
too much" said Hamlet
then she knew her fear.

What You Are Able

So again
you say
what it is
you say
same shit different
day because
that is all
there ever was
whenever you
would play
the minimum chips
barely wagered
and yet I stupidly
played and played
at the gambling
that you staged.

You want to cut
you want to
maim so now
I am All In
I will play your
game
you want to
hurt you want to
shame
you know what
you know
but if it is all
the same
two can play
blackjack though
my stakes are not
the blame.

I am not the dealer

-What You Are Able-

of jealousy
of afflictions
overbearing
interrogating
no I can play
at love I can risk
it all I can call
I can show
you my hand
never could
manage the bluff
yes now
all my words
are cut
in a huff.

You should stick
to roulette
you cannot hang
you cannot deal
you are paranoid
so suspicious
cannot see the
options while
trying to guess
placing cautions
within your chest
put your gun
to my head
I am on my knees
in your small
world betting
my chips I played
with ease.

Get over yourself
do not hedge the

-What You Are Able-

bet nothing is
able to get
your needs met
you wear your
pain like a
suit of armor
use it like
a poisoned
snake charmer
it is all so shiny
with a diamond
chain glimmer
a five and dime
sells the knockoff
and I am insane?

So, toss your cards
fold you are in denial
you are quite able
to go so now
you have been
told play the slots
it costs a lot
less you can
still call the shots
but fold and
get out that is what
it is about
you never sat down
with any real
clout.

Cookie cut a path
to your understanding
post a lucky piece
crowd commanding

-What You Are Able-

something from
2 years ago
when you tried
before
to win the bet
to win your loot
hit the craps
table grab dice
to shoot
get up and go
stay where you
know dump
the card table
you reap what
you reap
you will sow what
you are able.

Spit Forth Guts

Oh the venom
on these lips
cold fury should you
taste it there
quench your thirst
for my lies and
my truths my muted
thoughts.

Stand still frozen
dead in pools of wonder
and dread for this poison
that seeps into your
pores will not soon
leave the haunted spaces
your frightened places
there will be myriad traces
where it killed the
wonder it found in your
dull and dreary mind.

Choke on toxic thoughts
vomit my musings and
spit forth guts colored
black with doubt and
fear and torment stain
the ground with your
loosened purpose your
pathetic belief that
words are always intentions
of the noble and righteous.

Dismissed

You can now
never expunge me
banish me from
your view
delete me from
your life I
am the sentience
past and present
your decay
your debris.

I am black skies
above you
frozen ground
below you
I possess you
own you
you are
inconsequential
irrelevant
negligible.

No, you cannot
expunge me
I refute you
I banish you
I delete you
your presence
is hereby
eliminated.

You were nothing
to me mere
dust blowing in
the wind
a frozen planet

I tossed around
for my amusement
I am the Alpha
and the Omega
baby.

You will never
eliminate me
the poison of
my presence
has stained
your heart
love can never
again satiate
your needs
your desires
your longings.

I gorge on stars
eviscerate worlds
from my view
drain oceans
level mountains
you are puny
and that is
immutable
that is
irrefutable
so undeniable.

Gaze long
with dread into
the abyss that
is your pathetic
life
wail and cry

-Dismissed-

choke on the
reality that you
can never erase
me
ever retrace me
never replace me.

My dear
it is you who
is expunged
now blow away
you are nothing
your presence is
no longer required
you are
dismissed.

In Soft Tongues

You think fields are so lovely
you think as this snow falls
furious that it will give up
its words to the likes of
you. It would just go
speak to you in soft
tongues ones that
you alone you
only would
be able to
hear.
No
loud lies
no chance
will the snow
speak to or utter
to you than would
mighty Zeus himself
hasten swift down and
offer bolts of lightning of
which were long dreamt of
there was an eternity of need.

Tomb of A Room

I am thoroughly surprised
you chose the brocade
over chiffon my dear
poking at the brie
only serves to show
insolence and ignorance
and the violins give me
such a headache
such a migraine
jacketed like a
caterpillar in its
cocoon it is no wonder
it is difficult to breath
in this stagnant setting
this tomb of a room
we share but you knew
before the steaks
were cut that even
the strong breeze
from the open window
could not clear
this air didn't you?

Used To

She would say you
used to
pen little notes
to me
used to
text me
all the time
used to
make a nice
dinner on
some nights
and talk to
me for a while.

You
used to
tune into me
when I talked
used to
smile at me
used to
throw me
anywhere
and show
me why I
mattered.

I should have
told her why
but by then
retreat was
complete I
used to
drift to
where I would

imagine the
thoughts I
wanted to say
wanted to share
wanted to feel.

Where I would
talk about
forgiveness
letting go
moving past
perceived wrongs
and dead pauses
and bad timing
and change
and vagrant looks
and wrong choices.

But then
no matter
it was decided
always before I
ever decided
to stop the bleeding
I should have
said that she
never listened
never gave ground
to get beyond
her ugliness
her jealousies
her insecurities
her pettiness
her retribution
for a thousand
paper cuts

she said
I inflicted.

I should have
regrouped
come at it
a different way
no matter
she always decided
we should have
quit way back
when the
liquid band-aids
started this
theatre run.

Doomed
almost from
the start
all those lights
actors called in
scabs really
to play parts
which were
hastily sketched
around fragile love
not fleshed out
barely rehearsed
it is no wonder
that I
used to
and
that I
should have.

Malodor

A fragrance drifts
incessantly lifts
the hair on my neck
stiffens is it
reminiscent of lust?

I sense the odor
is in the jar...but
how then is it that
I smell it?

It being so far away
and yet
somehow seeping
all around me?

Incessantly creeping
this opiate from
a dark chamber
sleeps in Hamlet's
bed so that
a dagger seems
easier to love
than the smell of you.

Your Dead Horizon

Cold cloak chills
my aged bones
belies crimson eyes
those smoldering orbs
of despair and yet
I draw closer
I capitulate
I accede
in the knowing
of what is
and what will
never be
with one touch I am
asphyxiated
emasculated
entombed
my ashes barely glancing
your frozen ground
your dead horizon
your nuclear dust
before they are
pulverized and
obliterated
behind the echo
of your
terrifying laugh.

Seep Bone Coldly

No warrior's death is coming for me
no blood-stained sword will release
my foolish life from its hollow chest
stench of copper vile taste of metal
adrift I am alone and beaten and torn.

No quiet wake of honor shall be held
no slow loving march of the damned
terrible mists of doom rise eerily and
creep horrifically before my dying eyes
cast upon the distant shore of love lost.

No angels of mercy will soar this field
thick with the rancor of my bitter loss
shrouded by sick stench of stoic hope
not seep bone coldly into Hades cruel
might his dread hot abyss of suffering.

No arrow swift flying will find its mark
no sword nor spear will ever pierce me
I will wither and linger alone as it reigns
cold perfect terror over me and claws at
where slow my life leaking seeps to hell.

Therein

Therein lies your beauty
testify to me no longer
of dandelions and daffodils
of butterflies and bumblebees
do not chant as crows
beyond sight scatter
then gather
in frigid naked trees
diseased with
discord
disaffection
malfeasance.

The recompense for
transgressions
lays waste to beauty's cache
of finery
of magnificence
of splendor
do not disgorge sorrows
breathlessly
from your heaving chest
that conclave of muted
dreams vague and dreary
do not yearn
for lovely things
that
evade you
elude you
avoid you.

Talk then of
gnarled paths
overgrown with weeds
and thick brush

and rotting moss
sing soft melancholies
into indifferent airs
scatter your tributes
quick and breathlessly
entreat this soul
to yearn ache desire
for hues of sustenance
those colors
those images
those portraits
of secret truth
lying in wait
for the impact
of despair
dismay
distress.

Therein lies your beauty
your truth
and your essence
yet do not brave
the chasm for
it is conquered
it is besieged
it is occupied
by forlorn sages
aching to know
what chance their hopes had
from casting dreams
and illusions
and secrets
undetected
into blackened pools
of wonder.

-Therein-

Even dread Beelzebub
hot with rage
blindly jealous
with furious hatred
ravenous for vengeance
who rose
from putrid ashes
who rose
from rancid death
who rose
from deadly hell
fiercely intent on doom
is but feeble
and infirm
for scarcely could he
barely could he
set ablaze
reign terror
wreak havoc
on one tenth of
the thousand worlds
within this volatile
and eremitic imagination.

AFTERWORD

This is the first book in a 5 book Poetry anthology series titled Inexhaustible Life of Chaos. Angst and Anger is as much about pain and sorrow, rage and anger, as it is about loss and feelings of abandonment. The selection of poems for this anthology span over 30 years; yet a common theme emerges.

Whether it was unrequited love, a messy break up, or simply dealing with deep personal issues as they related to relationships; the theme is the same: my reaction to any form of rejection or perceived abandonment led instantly to poems of severe contempt or anger. My responses to lost love and failure at affairs of the heart speaks to my inability to balance emotions based upon reality. I felt too much and too often to be able to achieve some sense of homeostasis within myself.

I grew up very much a sensitive child who did not have his needs met, save for food and shelter. I think this had a profound effect on my ability to manage my emotions appropriately. As a result, whenever I experienced attraction or passion, I most always went too deep, too fast. For me it was simply all or nothing. There was no control valve for my emotions. No compass for me to follow. As a result, of course, I experienced painful incongruity between my perception of the emotions I was feeling, and their oftentimes opposite realities.

I am, myself, surprised at the theme that emerged once I chose the poems for this anthology. Though I have written countless poems, I had never once put them into any sort of theme like I have here in Angst & Anger. It has been an enlightening process. It has been almost cathartic as well: Answers to the deep mysteries of my overly powerful responses to people, places, and things, came into dramatic view.

Robert M. Levasseur

Made in the USA
Monee, IL
23 January 2021